Saint Francis of Assisi

A Life of Joy

Written by
Robert F. Kennedy, Jr.

Illustrated by
Dennis Nolan

HYPERION BOOKS FOR CHILDREN
NEW YORK

To Ena Bernard, who by her example, has taught my family all the virtues of Saint Francis

—R. F. K., Jr.

To Jan Baudendistel, who for eight years taught my daughter with understanding, joy, and love

—D. N.

First Edition
1 3 5 7 9 10 8 6 4 2

Reinforced binding
Printed in Hong Kong
Library of Congress Cataloging-in-Publication Data on file.
ISBN 0-7868-1875-1
Visit www.hyperionbooksforchildren.com

Saint Francis, for whom my father and I were named, was a kind of patron saint for my family. My first memory—I was one year old—is of sitting below a statue of Saint Francis with my father's black Lab, Charcoal, in the garden of the Georgetown home where I was born.

The next year we moved to Hickory Hill in the farm country of northern Virginia. Franciscan iconography decorated our home, and the garden bristled with shrines and statuary celebrating Francis and his friars.

As a born animal lover and the saint's namesake, I felt a special affinity for Francis. My bedroom walls sported more than forty framed pictures portraying events from his life. My mother and father read us stories of the "little flowers"—the followers of Saint Francis, whose devotion to God and His creation gave them a special relationship with the animals. Theirs were the primary virtues—courage, sacrifice, generosity, and love for the poor—that my parents sought to instill in their eleven children. I read every book I could about these noble men who embraced humility and poverty, served the vulnerable and sick, gave their lives joyfully in martyrdom, and saw every hardship as a gift from God.

Francis continues to be an important part of my life. My own garden in Mount Kisco, New York, has two shrines to Saint Francis. His stories line my bookshelf and scenes from his life adorn my office walls. I often visit Graymoor, the Franciscan monastery at Garrison, New York, for spiritual retreats. Just as when I was a boy, my prayers to Saint Francis are invariably answered.

Every night my wife and I kneel with our children around the bed to recite the prayer of Saint Francis together.

Lord, make me an instrument of your peace.

Where there is hatred, let me sow love;

where there is injury, pardon;

where there is doubt, faith;

where there is despair, hope;

where there is darkness, light;

where there is sadness, joy.

O Divine Master, grant that I may not so much seek

to be consoled as to console;

to be understood as to understand;

to be loved as to love.

For it is in giving that we receive;

it is in pardoning that we are pardoned;

and it is in dying that we are born to eternal life.

Francis understood that we need to love nature and spend time in it, because it is through His creation that the Creator communicates to us His grace and joy. Just as we know Michelangelo by looking at the Sistine Chapel, we know God best by looking at His masterpieces. And His finest work, arguably, was the little saint from Assisi, whose single aspiration was that his life be the perfect imitation of Christ's. After Saint Mary, Saint Francis remains the most popular saint in Christendom. He is also an ecumenical saint; even in his lifetime, he was praised as holy by both Christians and Muslims.

There are many wonderful stories of Saint Francis that I've left out of the book, and hundreds more about his followers: his extraordinary meeting, during the Crusades, with the sultan, who recognized Francis as a holy man; his reception of the stigmata of Christ, the bleeding holes in his hands, feet, and side that he would bear painfully until he died; his relationship with the peregrine falcon on Mount Alverna; his invention of the Christmas crèche; the many miracles associated with Francis's life; and the role of Francis and his followers in bringing to an end Europe's Dark Ages. I hope that this book will lead children to learn more about Saint Francis and to be inspired by the lessons of his life.

ASSISI, ITALY
Near the beginning of the thirteenth century

Late one night, the people of Assisi awoke to the sounds of boisterous laughter, music, and singing from the narrow streets of the medieval town. They shook their heads and covered their ears, yet most of them could not help smiling. Of course, the hilarious songs were the work of that charming rogue Francis Bernadone.

All Assisi knew Francis as the "King of Youth," the leader of an army of wild young men who were lavish with money and thought only of colorful costumes and crazy parties. He was a foolish rapscallion, but no one could stay mad at him for long because he was so charming and generous. Francis had black eyes and a kindly face, and he always seemed happy. His strong, musical voice could melt men's hearts. He desperately wanted to be a knight—fearless and pure of heart like King Arthur's knights of legend—or a troubadour, a traveling minstrel who composed poems and sang about love and chivalry.

Lord, make me an instrument of Your Peace

1

In Assisi, everyone loved Francis. He was famous for his manners and his unselfishness. He felt joy at his own good fortune and wanted to share his luck with others. As a boy, Francis vowed that he would give money to every beggar he met.

Francis's mother, Pica, taught him to love God and told him stories of the knights and their heroic deeds. She was proud of Francis for his kind heart. When Francis came home without his shoes or coat, she knew he had given them to some poor beggar. She noticed that Francis always put extra food on the family table, so that he could sneak off to share the leftovers with the poor.

Once when Francis was waiting on a wealthy customer in his father's shop, a ragged man came in to beg. Seeing that Francis was busy, the beggar left. When Francis finished selling cloth to the rich man, he locked the shop and dashed toward the marketplace, searching Assisi's steep, narrow streets until he was nearly out of breath. Finally, he found the startled beggar in the piazza and pressed into his hands the money from his last sale. Francis's father, Pietro, would have been furious if he had caught his son giving away money, clothes, and food to paupers. He was the richest cloth merchant in the city, and he loved to count his gold.

WHERE THERE IS HATRED, LET ME SOW Love

When Francis was twenty years old, war broke out between Assisi and the nearby city of Perugia. At last he could fulfill his dream of becoming a knight. Francis was the first of his friends to join the company of soldiers who fought with long spears called lances.

Francis fought valiantly at the battle of St. John's Bridge, but he and his fellow lancers were captured and thrown into a dark dungeon in Perugia. There he always shared his food and took care of sick prisoners. His jokes and laughter lifted the spirits of the men.

After a year in prison, Francis returned home a hero, but soon afterward he fell ill. One night, in a terrible fever, Francis had a vivid dream. He saw swords and shields in the shape of a cross. He took this to mean he should become a knight and fight for God. At that time, the Pope had called for knights from all over the world to fight the enemies of the Christian church.

The next day he bought a horse, armor, and a sword and rode off to join the Pope's war against the German king, hoping for military glory. But God wanted Francis to be a different kind of knight and struck him with a sickness that made him fall from his horse on his way to battle. Then God sent Francis a vision telling him to return to Assisi to learn the true nature of his knighthood.

Francis limped home filled with sadness. For weeks he rode the surrounding countryside wondering what he should do with his life. And then one day, he saw something he feared far more than battle or death. He saw a leper.

where there is injury, Pardon

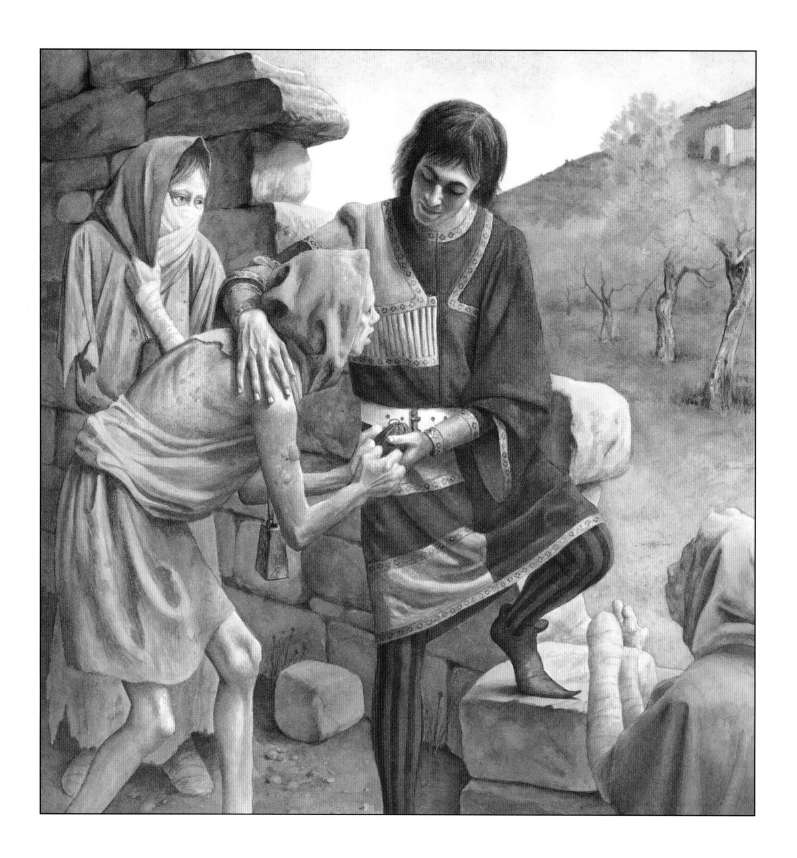

Although Francis was as lionhearted as the bravest of knights, he feared lepers. Francis couldn't bear the sight of these lonely, miserable derelicts, with their missing fingers, ears, and noses; their bleeding sores, their scabby faces. He was disgusted by the smell of their rotting flesh. It frightened him to think that just by being near them, he might catch their disease.

Lepers were made to live in the woods far from towns and to carry bells so people could hear them approach and run for their lives. If Francis saw a leper in the distance or heard those bells, he would turn his horse and gallop away.

On this particular day, Francis came upon a leper as he rounded a bend in the road. His first instinct was to flee. Then he scolded himself for adding to the man's misery. Instead of racing away, he dismounted. Gently pressing a bag of money into the leper's hand, Francis embraced the wretched man. A great happiness flooded his whole being.

Francis's deed had taken more courage than all his reckless bravery at the battle of St. John's Bridge. He was filled with such joy that he rode to a leper colony two miles from Assisi and begged the pardon of all the lepers. He kissed each of them and gave them his clothes and his money.

where there is doubt, Faith

Francis continued to wander the countryside looking for a mission to which he could devote his life. Each day during this period of seeking, Francis would pray in San Damiano, an ancient chapel half a mile from Assisi. One day he heard a voice. *Francis, do you see that my house is in ruins? Go and restore it for me.* Francis believed that this was a message from God, telling him to rebuild the dilapidated church.

Overjoyed to have a new vocation, he went home and sold his own horse and a bale of his father's best cloth to buy stones and mortar for the task. But his greedy father did not share Francis's enthusiasm for taking orders from disembodied voices—particularly when it cost him money. In a rage, he chained his son in a dungeon and beat him savagely, demanding that Francis return the money.

When Francis refused, his father dragged him to court before Bishop Guido at the bishop's palace in the central piazza of Assisi. All the townspeople filled the piazza, eager to watch a feud between the patriarch of one of Assisi's wealthiest families and his wayward son.

where there is despair, Hope

15

Bishop Guido was a wise and holy man. He admired Francis for his bravery and his love of God, but he told the boy to return his father's money. With that, Francis stripped naked and handed his father the money and his clothing. "Before this day," he announced in his strong, musical voice, "I have called Pietro Bernadone my father, but now I return his money and all the other things he has given me. Now God is my only father!"

Standing naked in front of the entire town did not help Francis's reputation. Just a few months before, the people of Assisi had considered him their hero. They had cheered as he rode out of town in glistening armor, vowing to fight for the Church and glory. When he returned a few days later, some people suspected he was a coward. Then he stole his father's cloth, and others thought him a thief. Now everyone was certain he was a lunatic. People laughed at him. Children threw mud and stones at him. He had become the biggest fool in Assisi.

Francis the fool marched naked from the piazza into the snow-covered woods. But instead of feeling sad and embarrassed, Francis was filled with joy. As the forest enveloped him, all Assisi heard him loudly singing the ballads of the troubadours.

where there is darkness, Light

A hermit gave Francis a tunic of rough cloth and a piece of rope for a belt. Francis dressed in this modest garb and went to live with the lepers, caring for them as he had before. When he returned to Assisi, it was as a beggar singing troubadour songs on street corners and pleading for stones instead of food. People laughed as they gave him stones and mortar, which he lugged downhill to repair the church of San Damiano. When generous folk threw him bread, he took only the hardest crusts or the stalest pieces, saving the choicer morsels for the lepers or other beggars.

Francis gave himself up to prayer, fasting, manual labor, and service with the same ferocity he had devoted to the adventures of war. He lived in the woods and called the sun and moon his brothers. He wrote beautiful poems and sang as he walked through the forests and fields. He made himself the poorest man in the world. But instead of being miserable, he became happier. "Blessed is he who expects nothing," Francis would later say, "for he will enjoy everything."

Many people thought he was crazy. But others began listening to his words.

where there is sadness, Joy

A wealthy nobleman named Bernard was the first to announce that he would join Francis in his life of poverty and service to others. Francis suggested that they seek guidance from God. After praying, they asked the priest to let his Bible fall open three times and read whatever he saw on the page before him.

The first passage said, "Go sell what you have and give it to the poor." The priest let the Bible fall open a second time and read, "Do not keep gold or silver or money in your purse, no wallet for your journey, and only one pair of sandals and a single tunic." The third passage read: "If anyone wishes to come to me, let him deny himself and take up his cross and follow me."

That very day, the two sold all Bernard's possessions and filled a large bag with gold coins for the poor.

A greedy priest named Sylvester saw Francis and Bernard giving away great fistfuls of gold to the happy beggars of Assisi. Squeezing through the crowd he shouted, "I gave you rocks for your church, but you never paid me!"

"Here you are," said Francis, handing Sylvester several gold coins from Bernard's bag. "If you want more, just say so."

The priest went home, feeling horror at his greed. That night, Sylvester's guilt would not let him sleep. He felt the gold coins like a great weight crushing his chest. The next day, he joyfully gave his own belongings to the poor and joined Francis and Bernard in the woods.

O Divine Master, grant that I may not seek so much to be consoled as to

Console

Within a few months, several men had joined Francis, including knights, priests, noblemen, a troubadour, a farmer, and a judge.

These men called each other "friar," meaning *brother*, and lived in simple huts made of branches and mud. They worked in monasteries or on farms, caring for lepers and giving all the money they earned each day to the poor, trusting in God to provide for tomorrow. They tried to live like Christ and His apostles, to carry nothing, and to find great joy in mingling with the sick, beggars, and other wretches. When they numbered twelve "brothers," they traveled to Rome to receive a blessing from the Pope.

As word spread about the friars, noble and courageous men in droves sold their belongings and followed Francis in poverty. Soon thousands of brothers were wandering all over Europe, serenading passersby with songs of joy. They ate roots and berries, performed good deeds, and comforted the sick. They could be seen on all the roads in Italy, Sweden, France, and Spain, walking two by two.

Just as King Arthur's knights had met once a year at the Round Table to share stories of their adventures, the friars would gather every few years in the forests and fields surrounding a woodland church that Francis had rebuilt from ruins, called the Portiuncula. There they rejoiced in God and prayed and ate together before scattering again across the land. Francis taught them that the Gospel, like the code of chivalry, required that they rejoice even when they were suffering, and that they should never complain and never blame anyone.

Happiness does not come from comfort or material possessions, Francis said, but from serving others. Francis reminded his friars that they should give to every beggar who asked. "If a thief steals your socks," he would tell them, "you should run after him and give him your shoes."

to be understood as to

Understand

23

Francis's example also inspired many women. One of these was Clare, a beautiful girl from a noble Assisi family. Her parents wanted her to marry, but she had a great yearning to give her life to the poor. She felt that her soul had been set on fire by the poetry of Francis's sermons.

When she was fifteen, she crept through a hole in the stone wall of her parents' castle garden with her cousin Pacificci, who also wanted to give her life to God and the poor. Friars with torches met the young women in the woods, where Francis cut off their hair before the altar of the Holy Angels and gave them rough tunics like his own. Then he led the girls to the monastery of the Benedictine nuns, two miles away.

Many of Clare's family members traveled to the monastery and vainly tried to persuade the girls to return. When Clare's younger sister Agnes made her own escape a week later, their fierce uncle Monaldo stormed the monastery with a dozen knights to capture the girls and bring them home. One horseman dragged poor Agnes by her hair over sharp stones down the rugged mountain path. "Help me, sister!" Agnes shouted to Clare. When Clare heard her pleas, she fell to her knees and prayed to God for help. Suddenly Agnes became so heavy that none of the men could move her even one inch more.

Although Clare was young, she inspired thousands of women to give up their worldly possessions and join in the life of poverty and service to others. This order of sisters became known as the Poor Clares. A great leader and a clever speaker, Clare could even persuade kings and princes to do her bidding on behalf of the poor.

In Clare, Francis had found a friend for life. Although they met rarely, they cared for each other and shared a deep love of God and nature.

to be loved as to Love

Francis loved animals and plants, the sea and the stars, and the beauty of the world that God gave us. He thought of God as a great artist who was best known through His creations. Francis believed that destroying any living creature was a sin against God and humanity, who benefitted from the joy and wonder that each creature inspired. He called all his fellow creatures "sister" and "brother."

He forbade friars to chop down living trees, and he would pick worms off the firewood to keep them from being burned. In the winter he brought warm wine and honey to the wild bees. Once he traded his cloak for two lambs that were being hauled to the butcher and allowed them to live out their lives at the Portiuncula. One of these devoted sheep followed Francis everywhere. It would kneel during Mass and always bleated respectfully when passing a statue of the Holy Virgin.

One day Francis said to his companions, "Stay by the road and wait for me while I preach to our sisters the birds." Francis walked to a nearby meadow, and as soon as he began his sermon, birds from every direction gathered around him to listen. They sat in silence even when his tunic brushed against them as he walked back and forth. When he finished, the birds showed their great joy by singing and spreading their wings.

Francis's life was filled with similar incidents. At Greccio, a hare followed Francis like a dog. When he was at Lake Rieti, a kingfisher and the fishes came each day to hear him preach, and a knight gave him a pheasant that stayed with him until he died. In the spring and summer evenings at the Portiuncula, a cicada would land in his hand when he called and sang with him.

For it is in giving that we Receive

Even fierce animals loved Francis, including the most ferocious of all, the wolf of Gubbio.

Once Francis visited the town of Gubbio, where the people could talk of nothing but a wolf of extraordinary size and appetite that was devouring their animals, as well as some men, women, and children.

Francis wanted to talk to this wicked wolf. Everyone begged him not to, but when Francis insisted, the people climbed atop the city walls for a better view. No one had ever seen a saint eaten by a wolf. (Even then, many people considered him a saint.) Men trembled and women screamed in terror when they saw the snarling animal charge Francis from the woods, its ravenous jaws wide, its teeth flashing.

But Francis made the sign of the cross, and the wolf came to a sudden stop. "Come here, Brother Wolf," Francis said. "In Christ's name, I forbid you to be wicked." Hearing this, the wolf dropped his head and lay at Francis's feet.

Francis scolded the wolf for its dreadful crimes and ordered it to stop eating the villagers and their animals. He promised to tell the people of Gubbio to not harm the wolf.

Miraculously, the wolf obeyed. For the rest of its life, the wolf lived peacefully in Gubbio—fed, cared for, and loved by the townspeople, because it reminded them of Francis's visit.

it is in pardoning that we are

Pardoned

Francis had lived a happy life serving others, acting as guardian to God's creatures, performing miracles, and inspiring men and women to devote themselves to poverty. Now Francis knew that his end was near, and he traveled the countryside on his donkey, urging crowds to love their fellow creatures. He was blind and suffered excruciating headaches and other illnesses and could rarely eat. Yet he was more cheerful than ever. Knowing that he would soon be in paradise with Jesus, his torments became a delight. It was at this time that he wrote his famous song "Canticle of the Sun," which praises the natural world that God created for our enrichment and enjoyment.

On his final day, Francis had himself taken from his hut and placed naked on the cold ground as a symbol of his life's work. Since the day when he had stood naked in front of all Assisi and given his life to God, he had not accumulated a single material object. He was returning to his God as he had entered the world.

As twilight enveloped the land, Francis saw his visitor coming. "Welcome, Sister Death!" he said joyfully. "It is you who will introduce me to eternal life."

Then, looking up, Francis saw God in all His glory. The stars that night, as they rose, gazed down upon the happiest man who had ever lived. At the instant of his death, a multitude of Francis's beloved larks descended on his hut and sang songs of great exultation.

All night the woods rang with the singing of the birds and of the friars who had camped there by the hundreds to bid Francis good-bye. Together they celebrated their great knight, whose life had been a love poem to God and Creation.

That evening, the earth and all its creatures had lost their greatest friend.

and it is in dying that we are born to

Eternal Life

Time Line

1182	Francis is born in Assisi and christened "Giovanni" (John). His father renames him "Francesco" (Francis), meaning "Frenchman."
1202	Francis fights valiantly but is captured with his fellow lancers during the battle of St. John's Bridge on the Tiber River, below Perugia.
1203	Francis is released a year later, and becomes a popular hero in Assisi.
1204	Francis equips himself as a knight and rides off to join the army of Pope Innocent III, in the Fourth Crusade. Sudden illness befalls him on the road to battle. In Francis's feverish vision, God instructs him to return to Assisi for another kind of knighthood.
1206	In the chapel of San Damiano, Francis hears a voice directing him to "repair my house which is falling in ruins." Although Francis humbly takes this direction to mean he should rebuild the ruined chapel at San Damiano, most Christians today commonly accept that he was called to become an example for the whole Catholic Church, which had become wealthy and corrupt. After Francis sells his father's cloth to help pay for San Damiano's restoration, his father has him dragged into court. Stripping himself of his worldly possessions, Francis enters the forest and commits his life to God.
1208	The first followers of Francis repent their sins and join him in the forest.
1209	Francis visits Rome with his twelve friars. Pope Innocent at first refuses to speak to the peculiar beggar. However, after dreaming that the ragged derelict, to whom he had earlier denied an audience, was holding up a toppling church, the Pope summons Francis and approves the friars' simple order embracing poverty.
1212	On Palm Sunday, Clare Scifi escapes her home and takes the vows of sisterhood before Francis. Francis makes his first attempt to visit Crusaders in the Holy Land. His ship is blown off course and he is stranded on the Dalmatian coast.
1213	Francis delivers his sermon to the birds near Cannara.
1214	Francis meets and kisses Saint Dominic at the Lateran in Rome. Their friendship inspires centuries of warm relations between Franciscans and Dominicans. At an annual "Chapter of the Mats," around the Portiuncula, 5,000 friars gather, and Francis calls volunteers to do their good works beyond the Italian border.
1218	By now friars are a common sight all over Italy, southern France, and Spain.
1219	Francis goes to the Holy Land and preaches first to the Crusaders and then to the sultan Al Malik Al Kamil, who offers him rich presents and begs him to remain in his court. When Francis refuses, the sultan gives him safe conduct through Muslim lands.
1221	Anthony of Padua joins the order, inspired by the deaths of five martyred friars in Morocco. Francis launches the "third order," opening the opportunity for lay and married people to commit themselves to Franciscan principles. Among the tens of thousands who joined over the following decades are Dante, Petrarch, Raphael, Michelangelo, Christopher Columbus, and other great thinkers who help revitalize the church and bring an end to the Dark Ages.
1223	Francis invents the first Christian crèche in a mountain cave near Greccio, where he celebrates Christmas Mass with hundreds of townspeople before a manger with cows and donkeys and sheep.
1224	Francis receives the stigmata on the summit of Mount Alverna.
1225	Francis writes "Canticle of the Sun," reciting it the first time for Sister Clare.
1226	Francis dies at the Portiuncula.
1228	Francis is canonized by Pope Gregory IX in Assisi.

The feast day of Saint Francis is celebrated on October 4 and the feast of Saint Clare on August 11.